KINK

MW00883875

NEW & SELECTED POEMS
Christopher Grosso

ISBN: 9798303088146

Acknowledgements:

These poems first appeared in the following publications:

APIARY

Arcadia Magazine

Blue Bonnet Review

Caesura

Gravitas

HOOT Review

Macrina Magazine

Sick Lit Magazine

Three Elements Review

Some poems in this collection were initially published in the Christopher Grosso's chapbook *Philadelphia Swank*, released by Thirty West Publishing as the 2017 winner of the Wavelength Chapbook Contest. Other poems first appeared in Christopher Grosso's chapbook, *Holes in the World*, released by Maverick Duck Press in 2022.

Other Works by Christopher Grosso

Novels

Mouth to God's Ear (Crossroad Press)

Mauled (Crossroad Press/Macabre Books)

Godfat's Door (Crossroad Press/Macabre Books)

Odor of Sanctity: A Tale of Stigmata (Forthcoming, 2025)

Poetry Collections

Philadelphia Swank (Thirty West Publishing, Wavelength Award Winner)

Holes in the World (Maverick Duck Press)

Said to Godhead (Alien Buddha Press)

WTF, Enjoy: Poems from Marc Maron's Newsletter (Forthcoming, 2025)

For Greg

.

Table of Contents

HOLES IN THE WORLD

A friend is digging
a giant hole in his backyard
for lack of anything else
to prove progress.

His wife worries it is his grave.
He worries it is too.

We visit, watch him drive
the shovel tip into the soft,
damp earth, the vestibule
of decomposition.

He's gone down
up to his ears now,
his crow-footed eyes
level with the ground.

We grab a shovel to help,
but he stops us, says
that we dig our own holes
in this world. We disagree.
The world digs them for us.

GERM OF A STORY

Young Hemingway returned
to his parents' home
from the war and needed
to sleep with the light on,
fearing the dark would carry him
to death in its humid womb.
Reading Life magazine
till lights out, he'd flick the lamp
off and quickly back on,
recalling his days during the war
when he drove an ambulance
that took what was left
of young men from the front
to the rear, often leaving pieces
of them behind to marinate
in dark puddles of bomb waste.
They left lips that only lied
about kissing. Fingers
that never sunk into a woman's
warm heaven. Legs that
had just danced at a prom.

He said that, in the ambulance,

men told all secrets.

They spilled their guts,

screaming to some father

for forgiveness of such boring

adolescent sins.

If the morphine

could not dampen their screams,

he turned out the light

in the ambulance and told them

story after story of parades

in the States for war heroes,

complete with pretty girls

who just love stumps.

When they quieted,

he turned the light back on.

ACTIVE DYING

In apocalyptic fiction,
the world as we know it
ends, while a few characters
get to go on. You go on
with the survivors,
follow along with them
through a story
of the end as the beginning.

Dying is the opposite.
You end, the world goes on.

Everyone is a survivor
in this apocalyptic story
but you. Your story ends.
Except, you are not a story.
You can't be.
Stories cannot be terrified
that they are about to end.
Stories don't scream
as the last line is written.

SEMI-HARD COCKAMAMIE

The body under the bloody white

sheet on the street is a corpse.

But not I. I shall never corpse. Nor rot.

I've been written.

I've been written as a great theology.

A composition composed.

Who can decompose the written?

The unwritten cannot. The unborn can't.

The unalive are the aren't.

These things are the absence.

There is no theology in absence.

Nothing and no one to argue

against or for. Empty as dark.

With no light to see your opponent,

you would just sit there,

slapping yourself in the face.

Just an academic exercise

of masturbation

with brass-knuckled hands

on your semi-hard cockamamie.

No, I've been written as a great theology.

A conquistador's tale

of conquering hell, heaven, legend.

Devils colonized to a bowing civility.

Mermaids tanked in aquariums.

Angels on leashes.

The angels are grounded.

Flightless. They are rewritten flightless.

Now it cannot be unwritten.

The angels are revised to sit still

forever and ever.

Despair, rewritten into the text.

Or oblivion, rewritten on a sheet.

On the street. Over a body.

In that dreaded red.

Copied over my great theology.

Revision of my theology.

Rewritten out of existence.

The wordless prayer.

Wordlessness writ on the heart.

The wordlessness of existence.

THE WIND CANNOT GET LOST

Who can hum joyful hymns
when the boss is staring at you
with indifference from the end
of the long mahogany
conference table?

I will keep this short:
I am not worth
the price of the cigarettes
that are killing me.

No myth of myself.
Not chasing anything,
I am nonetheless winded
and steal breath,
air that would be better
used by others.

Still, sitting still, I must sit
at the conference table
and age an hour or two
looking at my boss

looking at me, reminding myself

that I don't really want to die tonight,

but instead get drunk

tonight till I reach a moral lobotomy.

Tonight, each night,

I am a coward walking home,

one who would walk this life

with my eyes closed,

but I am too afraid of the dark.

Thankfully, like the wind,

I cannot get lost.

Though I am not the wind,

I am just a puff of stale air,

capable only of knocking

over empty bottles

not whole liquor stores.

I not only lack the courage,

but a getaway car too.

If I had a car,

I wouldn't getaway,

I'd get into the race,

I tell myself,

walking home on a breeze.

LIFE, MID-COUNTY

What can I say? Sometimes a novel
turns out unexpectedly bad while your life
turns out pretty good. For your literary
legacy as the tortured genius,
I know you hoped it would've been
the other way around. But even when
the bills are paid, the dog fed,
and the oven self-cleaning, you can still
take off your starched shirt
at the Thanksgiving Day dinner table
and beat your chest violently, pointing
at the scar over your heart where
your now-removed biker tattoo
used to scare children and small puppies.

SYMPOSIUM

The day is just old,

gray, loose skin,

as the speaker pushes

and pulls himself uphill,

from sleepy wisdom

to tired jokes,

and exhausted

like a salmon

squirming upstream

in tough instinct,

flopping through

the constant being of the verb's

low hum near rest.

His words are colored sluggish,

drawn in long,

thick strokes

and smudges of inconsequence.

In an escape window,

the sun is

too espresso

to consider,

the sky

too blue-eyed

to long for,

especially when the

ever-waiting ceiling

is a boxed

plaster lid over

some expiring food

— we are the hardened pastry,

our minds are cold decaf coffee —

the day is

four walls

oozing with slow.

NOTICE THE NOT

Bottomless body, Cassandra called my
nearly non-existent ass the first few weeks

of our newly shared nudity. Flat in back,
from cranium to Achilles. Kansas ass,

the great plains, the boardroom table,
she'd say, giggling. A pimple would be

a noticeable convex improvement.
Thank goodness for suspenders

or you'd be dropping drawers more
than an arthritic bureau maker,

she commented, flush with white wine.
Cheek implants had been discussed,

but the cost was prohibitive. So my ass
will remain as it is — a rear end in

function only, without any aesthetic
value, an ugly machine void of

beauty. Even worse, my ass is now
too common to comment on, as the joke

about my leveled ass has become
worn out, been forgotten and replaced

by new chiding and kidding about
more timely subjects of life. Cassandra

no longer notices my ass now that she sees
it every day. Even for what it lacks, she

has ceased noticing what it could be.
Soon my hands will vanish while touching

her breasts, my legs will disappear when
kneeling before her, begging her to

never stop making fun of my heart
for being so big and so obvious.

THE SECOND DATE WITH CASSANDRA

Without a moment's warning,

just as my mouth

opened ever so slightly,

I sneezed

with a mouthful

of half-chewed almonds.

I've never before seen

a tree explode.

I assumed you had not either,

sitting across from me.

You didn't recoil

from the barrage,

or scrunch your cute nose

in disgust, opting

to instead pause,

survey the wet chunky sawdust

that pebbled

your porcelain smooth arms,

the gritty confetti

cascading down your lush hair,

and say how fortunate

that I did not have

a mouthful of

harsh words,

stories of fleeing.

FOLLOWING FOOTSTEPS

My father wore a necktie
to the office

each day. A perfect
Windsor knot

shuffled tightly against
a starched white collar.

I could never achieve
the Windsor.

Its twists and loops
escape me.

PENMANSHIP

He was an admirer
of Kerouac's liver.
That of Faulkner's, too.
He dug the penitentiary mind
of Burroughs, all walled up
with excuses and denials.
Wanting the fists of Bukowski,
the gonzo of Thompson,
the hunts of Hemingway,
he once attempted to
shave a cactus at a party.
The prickly spines
resemble cheek stubble,
he mused, so logic seemed
to be smiling on his quest
like sun smiles on a
Sunday afternoon soiree.
It was a Sunday afternoon,
as a matter of undisputed fact.
It was sunny. The orange juice
was infused with Russian water.

The air held the sharp end

of the weekend. His pen

was down. His razor was up.

The cactus won handily,

his bloody digits did attest.

"A bearded dragon," he called it.

"Get my sword," he yelled, "I will

slay the mighty beast."

In the hard Monday morning dawn,

after the mind-wet guests had gone

home to wring themselves dry,

the cactus turned out to be

just a rose. Just a mighty red ask

for love, forgiveness, memorial.

IN HOLLOW BONES

Airport baggage handlers
do not speak of guilt.
The metaphor is too
burdensome on the back.
Besides, they know
what is in your bags.
Without even looking,
they know what you've
stowed: sex toys on a
business trip — they know why!
Undeclared fruit — they can
almost taste it. Conch shell
from a protected beach —
they can hear the ocean
through the bag.
And they don't judge.
They simply move the bag
from conveyor to cart to
plane belly. They leave it
in the belly. Let you carry it.
Let you carry it up

and away. The hollow bones
of a plane filled with your you,
take flight. Carry your bags
and your metaphors
somewhere else, they say.
Just not here. We know bags.
The bags don't stop coming.
Day and night, relentless,
we do not speak of that.

MATRICULATION

The new adults barely dress.

Skin is worn like clothes.

There is no shame to cover up yet.

Ambitions are too hot. Life goals are raw footage,

unedited. Bare to the world,

naïve enough to believe something done,

doing, will do, will matter.

That their actions will have a consequence

on the world and no consequence to them.

Nothing hurts except when the night must end.

The inactivity of rest is the only nuisance.

Their color is blue-flamed new fire.

Fireworks burst from their mouth

when speaking their mind.

Every day is their birthday that they love to count.

Everything is addition. Everything is spice

from some exotic orient.

What's this word, 'tepid?'

Does it mean you, they think?

They spot them on occasion. Now and again

they see one. They can spot them

by the slumped shoulders and muted dress

and briefcases weighted with medicine.

You are not rare creatures — a species

afraid of the sun and lulled by the dark to sleep.

What is this they are feeling, they wonder.

What is this strange new word?

This, they believe, is how you spell pity.

SOME NEEDS NEED

As often as

masturbating, in private,

people who wake

before the alarm clock

try to imagine what it

would be like to be dead.

Be unlike alive.

Like no simile,

unable to compare

something against nothing.

No you no more.

Not feeling

even the unfeeling.

Being un-being.

Until the mind, pushing

inward against itself,

till the world

in the mind,

swells, implodes,

comes to grips

with the hand of time.

WOMEN ARE FORBIDDEN FRUIT
THAT MAKE MANY JAMS

and deathtraps —

her hair smells fine,

like lime and coffin upholstery.

Or maybe it's the muse dying,

like Picasso's ear

rotting on some dame's bookshelf.

Or cupid's dirty diaper

gone putrid, or a container

of used elbow grease

wasted on a poem,

a love letter gone rancid

in a Philadelphia trashcan

like a jar of strawberry aphrodisiac.

I only dance with a girl to prove

that my legs work and I won't fall down,

but the music suddenly stops

and I stare at the girl. I stare

in a moment of social hemlock.

Even before I run across the room

and throw the punch bowl on the floor,

I know the morning's regret

— when the sins of the night

greet the morning light —

when the evidence of some bouncer's beating

spreads from dimple to dimple,

broken teeth falling from my mouth

like hail in hell. I find myself retracing

my steps home at dawn,

find a petal beneath my dance shoes,

a sober grace beneath my heel,

one minute for a love metaphor,

and only one hour to get to work.

AT SENTENCING, THE PRAYER

God, I swagger through your
soft anger. Your expressions
of distaste are too easy to cover
in cupcake icing, which just adds
to my warming fat for winter.
I reinterpret your tiny wraths
as exfoliation of my venial,
venereal sins. Your cold bath
is so invigorating, so sudsy,
I blow your bubbly clouds
around my sea, getting ready
to sail again. Or drive in circles,
hitting the same potholes
I dug yesterday. So, you gavel
a sentence against me — to again
lose my car keys. I can still
get home. You can't help yourself
but provide tokens of mercy,
everyone on the bus will tell you.

CASSANDRA, THE DEFINITION OF GOOD LIVING

is just

making a name for yourself

somewhere that matters

to trophy engravers.

Cassandra, I have no trophies.

My name is C —

and I am a 45-minute drive

from Philadelphia swank.

I'm even further from

wanting to go there.

And even if I'd won a trophy,

my name is too obscure for posterity,

too illegible beyond the boundary

of our custom doormats.

See, my friends have moved

too far away. They've packed

their cars full of trophies and

moved around the block

to a cul-de-sac called Successful.

Though the success of friends

bitters my sweet tooth, I know

that in a crowd of successful people,

my successful friends become as nameless

as C —, like an expensive car

surrounded by expensive cars

all driving uptown.

Cassandra, do you understand

what I'm driving at?

Steer clear of me because

even though this poet wants

an expensive car too

(shiny and new), I want

to drive it without looking

until the car gets dented perfectly original.

Cassandra, the dents are what

will make the car mine.

HANDLING

I seek advice from my car
because it can control things

like stopping, how far you
can recline back, the speed

at which it moves forward.
"How can I replicate this feat

in my life?" I ask the car.
The only reply I receive

is about engineering: curves
of mathematics arcing across

a blueprint into steel joined
by torqued craftsmanship.

Precision planning, it tells me,
from the initial pillar of the frame

to the showroom-sparkling
fender. That's how you assemble

control, it says. I look at myself
in the rearview mirror. Crow's feet,

sore back, sighing regret. I was not
built for driving the blind curves

of this dark uphill road. "I've not
planned where I am going," I say,

and stomp my foot on the car's neck.
It jumps, screeching to my will.

19TH CENTURY ETERNAL

for Emily Dickinson

If you had tasted

the copper coins

that covered

you father's dead eyes,

you would have

known why some men

are called the 'salt of the earth.'

Why the coins

are always cold to the touch,

salty to the tongue.

Why the salt of the earth

must melt the ice

that keeps the corpse fresh.

The salt gives grip

so we won't slip on the ice

into despair.

He was cold to you.

You kept your footing.

SAINTS, MID-COUNTY

The noise from the vacuum cleaner
the cute barista is brandishing as I try to
read Daniel Berrigan poems reminds me
that homicide is possible. An option, like
skim or whipped cream, hacksaw to the neck
or acid into the fizzy water the barista sips
between swipes of the roaring sweeper.
I could do it and still taste heaven one day.
There are saints who committed murder,
then lamented by tearing their clothes,
smearing themselves in ash, sporting
sackcloth until redeemed like a coupon.
This is suburbia, however. The ingredients
for that recipe do not exist where the shelves
are too fully bare of lepers' rotted limbs,
and no one is being fed to lions
or tasting the lash. Suburbia has never
produced a bona fide saint. The shelves
here are too full of cake mix, molasses, and
other sludge of thick rush. Here, a husband,
guilty for lusting after a sweet barista can

rush home with roses for his wife. She can ignore the thorns and ease his throbbing.

"It is getting late," I yell to the barista above the vacuum's roar. "I should get home."

TINY HOLES

You can't help

but look at the deformity

of automotive steel

married to a tree trunk

along the side of a windy road.

A steering wheel

lost up in an elm.

Of blood cocktailed with sap.

Human weight scattered

about in tiny ounces.

You think, cube steak!

Then feel criminal.

Cleanse off with a tiny prayer.

Squeeze out platitudes

from your mind like you're

making lemonade from lemons.

Look away. See a squirrel

with an acorn in its mouth.

Its tiny hands quarrying

in the dirt. It makes a tiny hole.

Drops the acorn inside.

Fills in the hole with dirt.

You think of burial, of course.

Oblivion. Then the squirrel runs

into the street without looking.

GRANT APPLICATION FOR NEW CONSTRUCTION

All construction is new.

Otherwise, it would be a deconstruction.

Or demolition. New, in this usage, is redundant.

Avoiding that redundancy is the accuracy

of language that we will achieve at this college

when we build this new building.

What we are building is growth.

This place is going places. Upward and out.

Like in puberty, we can't stop growing.

We need to be fed constantly.

The rumors are true. We don't even need

to mention how well we are endowed.

The college is a phoenix rising from

the other phoenixes. Separating from the pack.

Galloping ahead. Thoroughbred. Transcending.

The building will house our best and brightest.

From downtown, your inner circle will see the glow.

From your offices downtown, you can point at it.

The whole city will know what you've done.

When you see what will happen inside

this building, you'll epiphany all over yourself.

Other colleges will whimper in submission

when they see what you've done. They'll look at you

and see a pillar. A monument to monuments.

They'll see what you're capable of. They'll know.

What this building will teach is knowing.

Knowing is all they need to know.

We'll show them. We'll show them all.

Show them just what we're made of.

What we're made of will have made the building.

We're stronger than the brick that made the building.

We'll be able to look at the brick and not genuflect

with the rest of them. We can say "new construction"

if we choose to say it. Just imagine.

We'll be able to say anything we'd like.

FEARS OF MEN

The fears of men leave a greasy smear

on the ground trailing behind them.

For a while, they are bears attacking a beehive,

ravaging the honeycomb for just

a small taste of something so powerful

that they are raptured into forgetting

why their hands shake, lips quiver.

The bees' stingers make holes

in the heated men, and sizzling fat drips

through the holes, leaving

an inelegant stain on the carpet.

That's how it gets there.

Spring after spring of bee stings.

Men squeal in delight, rolling on their backs.

Men do not need a carpet

to roll around. They got fat for that.

They growl and do it on the ground.

Pigs in shit. Bulls in China shops.

They only stop at God. Or rather

the immobility of meeting God.

Of stopping eternal. Just the thought

makes men throw things in the air —

footballs, rockets, fireworks, fingers.

This is praise. This is the tongue men speak

in and about. An explosive theology

of castrated desire. With age,

the dos of this and the don'ts of that

metastasize to everything till men sit

in the rocking chair, doomed. They know

even the chair is doomed to stop rocking.

THE STRANGE SPEAK

My Latin

is a rusty crucifix.

Deus Caritas Est. "God is Love?"

Or maybe,

"God is Established?"

Erected like a tall

walking bridge to no place,

built just for people

to jump to their deaths.

Or maybe

to their afterlife.

That bridge exists.

Just south of Weston.

Or maybe east of Northumberland,

near a sleepy village

where the children throw

rocks at the stained glass

windows of the church,

and the bridge is old, curmudgeonly,

smudged with copper-colored

badges of rust.

Or maybe

it is dried blood

from all of the jumpers

hitting the steel pylons

on their way down

toward the lapping water.

Or maybe

the water is not lapping,

but laughing

in some tongue we

don't understand anymore.

Only the fish can understand it.

Or maybe only the kids skipping rocks

can understand it.

Or maybe

the kids in town throw rocks

at lost strangers,

herding them toward the bridge,

edging them off the bridge

with sticks and stones.

The children speak a strange language.

We used to speak it.

Now we speak about bridges.

It's a strange Latin. Rusty words.

Or maybe not.

WAKING UP WITH STIGMATA

Hold up one of the

hands to the light.

Look through the hole

in the hand. Wonder.

Stick a finger

through the hole.

Wiggle the finger.

Move the finger

back and forth

in the hole.

Hang a hanger

in the hole. Swing

the hanger side to side.

Hold up the other hand

to the light. Look

through the hole

in the hand. See.

Put the barrel of a gun

through the hole.

Next, a pencil.

Try to write

with the pencil

sticking out of the hole.

Put both hands together,

palm to palm,

and see if you can

stick the pencil

through both holes.

If you can, try to snap

the pencil in half.

Stick your tongue

through the hole.

Place your hands on

the mirror. Look

through the holes.

See yourself

through the holes.

Hold up one hand

to the light.

Look through the hole

in the hand. Know.

Kneel down. Palms

on the ground. Get

dirt in your holes.

NO OBITUARY

No one will ever write a biography
about you. You will go unaccounted
into no posterity. The only you
that will ever be is you now.
Just you, sitting at the foot
of the bed, listening to your wife
snore. Just you, in the early hours,
bemoaning in stifled grumbles
of morn the day's coming tasks.
Just you, trying to caffeinate
to face the inconsequence of today.
Sipping coffee. Not screaming.
Just you, throwing the coffee mug
across the room at the wall.
It doesn't even break. Just ricochets
back toward you. You look at it
there on the carpet, unbroken.
The mug has one word written on it.
Just one word. A very short word.
It doesn't matter what the word is.
You crawl back into bed. Your wife

wakes at the commotion. You tell her you're skipping work. "But you'll be written up," she says. "They will write you up for it." You just snore.

THE ONLY LIST THERE IS

Do not fold your hands in prayer.
They are dirty hands. Your hands

may look clean, but they are filthy
with sweaty grime from making fists

when standing up in your coffin
and facing death head-on, man to man

eye to eye. That holy water is not
for cleaning your soiled hands.

It is God's spit. Have your mother
put a bit on her finger and wipe

a smudge of ketchup off of your face.
Or is that blood? No matter!

The holy water is a sign to remind you
to look for signs. Not signs of the end

times though. The end isn't near
because it has been here all along

on the dotted line where your mom
signed your name at birth. You love

her for signing you up on life's list
of the doomed. It was the only list

she could sign your name on.
You can't blame her. Remember,

it is the only list there is, and the list
looks like an unraveled prayer anyway.

KINKED EXISTENCE

In the beginning, our species
would walk sideways, leaning over.

We were being blown this way
and that by the breath of God

when he kept whispering, "Fall."
We were crooked from the start,

which is why the bent fetal position
is the first we each hold

when we are dreamt up from non-existence.
For a while there, we shambled around

like we were each a Leaning Tower of Pisa.
We were walking so cockeyed that God

tilted the world on its axis to straighten
us out and give us some damn dignity.

Then in our mania at being fully upright,

we tore off our fig leaves and lay together,

limbs all slippery knotted. Now, sometimes,

the ground shakes beneath our feet.

Orgasm. Earthquake. Shakespeare.

We can hardly walk after. We're all crooked again.

After exposure to these shifting tectonics

in our loins, land, and language, we never

feel secure on our two feet.

We know then that we're supposed to lean.

That the correct way to look at the world is sideways.

SERMON MAKING

First, the sermon cannot be
a stagnant pond, too still for the even
the stagiest teetotaler to tolerate.

But don't make waves either. Just hang
a rope swing inviting enough to
skip work to try. Now, your words

should not become manufactured steel
but be blacksmith original, fitted per request,
each tune tuned for the tone-deaf ear.

Bring your saber, but only as a prop.
Place it gently before you. No need
to rattle it as the import is tariff enough.

Then finger paint in the air while speaking,
keeping the colors hot. Do not be afraid
to point at the flock, letting them know

they are both counted and accountable.
Most importantly, hold out your hands
in blessing, saying, "Can you see what

I am offering you? Just my empty,
wanting hands, reaching out, waiting
to squeeze your doubt into diamonds."

ACCOLADES

O ambition,

you tire

like a kitten

swimming

in milk.

OUR PUDDLES

The so few faces we show,

we know we stroll through

the day in some way not entire,

just some profile

still less-than half the whole.

Let's face it,

we have faces that even

we cannot face.

So in an abundance of lotion,

we lather ourselves slippery

for the world to not hold on,

to see not.

Time-lapse photos of time

lapsing us we see in mirrors,

so yes we spackle, adorn to pretend.

We pretend for others

and pretend not to pretend,

as they do too, clowns

in a circus of believe-not.

In time, time downpours

and rains away what we

could not reign in no matter

the time it takes to face inward,

as is the point pointing

to our soggy crescendo.

Less-is-more is more-or-less untrue,

we say, looking down

at the rainy mirror in our puddles.

LET'S BE NOT BLESSED

Let's invite sin to be voluminous tonight, thick with decadence.

Let's martyr the chaste, the moderate taste.
Turn the bland into firecrackers.

Let's loot the confessional for testimonial,
for inspiration from the dark below.

Let's go rodeo on one another, get rambunctious
with riffraff and make a go at a go-go.

Let's plunge our minds to find the filthiest wish,
the devil's kiss, the brush with death defy.

Let's toss aside the loveless task,
the steel mask and other locks of life.

Let' follow the quickened pulse, the tensed tickle in our noggin.

Let's say no, no, this time, say yes, the blessed-be will be.

Let's walk through the valley of tears wearing nothing but our
decadence, naked and blunt for the world.

I RECALL OLD WINTERS

"Blade, hoe, manhood—
What have my tools to do with what wakes in her."
-Daniel Berrigan, SJ

Heather, my hands crack
in the cold each winter.

Thin little cracks
of skin on the knuckles,

broken open and bleeding from
rough long exposure to unfriendly elements.

My hands can look like
they belong to some street boxer

after a brawl with deep self-torment
in an alley behind a longshoreman

whiskey joint in Northeast Philadelphia.
Which of course they do belong to,

though they do not ache with regret.
No, my hands are not guilty Macbeths.

Even if they need to shovel
new graves in potter's field

for a paycheck they will, for you,
they will dig for deep metaphor.

But our life requires no lyrical tools
to construct its meaning. Quite simply,

my hands cannot handle the winter.
I feel spring blooming and my hands

are beginning to heal. My hands
are healing for our springtime.

HEAVEN A BORE

What if I don't like heaven?
If it doesn't appeal to me?
What if I don't like the people
there? I suppose it wouldn't be
heaven then. But I know some
good people who I detest
and I know some bad people
whose company I quite enjoy.

Let's be honest now: Do-gooders
can be quite boring people.
I don't want to spend eternity
with the squeaky clean,
the polished pure, doing
the right thing always.

A little bit of sin is exciting.
Nothing major
– just little naughty moments.
I hope I can have a little sin in heaven.

ACTIVE DYING II

After they first told me I was dying,

for many days I was expecting the Doc

to tell me the whole damn dying-thing

was a gag.

He'd come into my hospital room,

a shit-grin on his face,

holding back his amusement,

until he put his hand on my shoulder,

finally letting his laughter loose.

"We sure did get you,"

he'd say. "You old gullible sonofabitch you!

You believed the whole damn thing. Dying!

And you believed us!"

Then for the rest of the day

the nurses would stop by my room,

a small smile on their young faces. "It was

so hard to see you all these days, to keep

the joke going and not laugh.

The Doc sure got you good."

I'd laugh too, being able to take a joke.

When I saw the Doc

on the golf course the next week,

I'd laugh with him again.

"You sure did get me, Doc. You got me good.

Damn funny, it was." We'd tee-off

in a foursome, play a few holes

on a perfectly sunny spring day.

He'd make a birdie, pars,

an eagle, and finally

another joke about his death-gag.

I'd smile, raise my club above my head

and scream, "It isn't fucking funny anymore."

I SWEAR

that miracles exist

because it has to be a miracle

that we don't more things

stuck in our eyes.

We've got these exposed

soft round sacks of fluid

sitting in our heads

and we walk around a hostile world

wide-eyed through blustering winds

full of cigarette-ash twigs bugs dirt sand

and we rarely get scratched scraped

or punctured in the eye.

We scrunch wink blink

and bug-out our eyes,

we bend over dropping our heads

toward an untied shoelace,

we whip our eyed heads around

when we hear our names,

we bob our wobbly heads

to music completely drunk

and off-balance,

yet the eye seems to remain

safe, secure even cozy beneath

hardly protective lashes.

The eye gets bloodshot teary

and sometimes itches, produces

eye boogies and gets shifty

when lying. But the eye survives,

stubbornly looking into burning buildings

for survivors, looking at a calendar

with hope for tomorrow, looking into

another person's eye to see

if all the great clichéd cosmic wonder

of connection is truly shared,

if somewhere beneath all the social aphorisms

and quick pairing of equivalents

we find something delicate

that actually survives, one thing that holds

 the entire universal ugliness in a frame

and still stares into the blank antimatter

of reality and says, "Look, I can see faith."

TO A PHYSICIAN FROM A PRIEST

You've seen innards.
Exposed intestine,
tendrils woven like goopy lace.
Held inert hearts
just extracted and exerted
them to twitch a bit,
soon throb and pump gain.
Patient packed tight,
sewn shut, they call you
their savior.

Perhaps I am jealous.
Some humility overwhelmed
in my chest beneath
where my crucifix hangs
because I know you fix
the acute cases now,
achieve wellness so tangible
you can almost hear the joy
in the heart-monitor's beeps.

You see results

within moments, hours.

I can only wait for heaven

and hope to see souls I've worked.

Just one soul would suffice.

One soul fulfilled, whole,

thrilled at seeing yet

another sunrise

in eternity's light.

GOD PENS A POEM ABOUT US

I leave you alone for one eternity
and the place is a mess.

If you want justice,
sit in my chair and stare
at what you've done:
making tanks instead of toys,
battalions not balloons.

You wonder why you live instead of doing it,
asking about the end like the last word
in some simple sentence.

Here are simple sentences for you:

Manure makes fertilizer.
Fertilizer makes flowers.
Bees make honey.

Can I be any clearer
than a sunny day without your smog?

Pick up those toys and start playing.

Believe in make-believe.

Your seriousness is a snooze.

Stop putting manure in your honey.

That shit is sweet enough without your toying.

ON POSTHUMOUS APPLAUSE

Shave off all of my body hair
after I die and make a bird's nest
for a pterodactyl who mates a Pegasus.

Scalp my skin clean-off
and make a sail of it
fit for a pirate ship
dragging with booty.

Bring back boneyards with mine,
and put my eyes on the ass
of a stubborn donkey
that walks backwards near a cliff.

Let my heart sump-pump
a grandma's cellar where yesteryear
greeting cards are forgotten to rotten
in an old, powdered milk box.

Just don't bury me in applause
please or the gods will scream
bloody murder.

I DON'T DATE
LIT PROFS ANYMORE

because when

arguing one night

when I was drinking

too much sloe gin

too fast

in my old birthday suit

on the new couch

she said that

I'm just like

a Bukowski poem.

So, I thanked her.

She marked me

as absent

and I still passed,

colors flying.

SUMMER MUSE

I love

seeing girls

in short

poems.

TRUTH, THUS SAYETH

slant, or roundabout
to get home. Nothing
purgative is straight
and narrow to the
unlocked front door.
Narrator, sayeth this:
A drunk cannot walk
a straight line nor
speak a convincing lie.
There is a truth
muddled somewhere
in there like a cocktail.
In the slurred
mumbles, the reckless
dance home from the
corner stool, the path is
not direct. It is though
well-trod from fresh shod.
Thus sayeth a gospel,
that all news is not good.

THORNS OF MERCY

Mercy, she says,
is a word only employed
by the powerful,
the landed gentry, she says,
holding a plow over our
plot of mortgaged earth
to plant more red roses
in our botanic abundance.
The thorns are a mercy too,
she says, looking at
a pinprick droplet of crimson
blood resurrecting on her skin.
That's a wet leveling, she says,
a renaissance of reminder
that we too are needful
of some sun, warmth,
a sacramental drop of water
on the lashing tongue.
Blood is made of water,
she says, and much more
that cannot be seen by

our naked eyes. Same as

mercy, she says, that we

hold in us, deep and powerful

to the last drop.

THE LAST DROP

The slick punches come quick
when you cannot duck
behind the inebriate waterfall.
No water no more. Just the fall.

The telltale bruises a hieroglyph,
time a blackened reminder
of how dark forgetting can be.

It isn't the punches that hurt
the worst, but the tomorrow
that always begins with the

sorrow, the sorry, of yesterday.

Christopher Grosso is the author of the novels, *Mouth to God's Ear*, *Mauled*, and *Godfat's Door*, all published by Crossroad Press/Macabre Books. His previous collections of poems include, *Philadelphia Swank* (Thirty West Press' "Wavelength Award" Winner), *Holes in the World* (Maverick Duck Press), and *Said to Godhead* (Alien Buddha Press). Forthcoming is his novel in dramatic form, *Odor of Sanctity*, and his collection of found poems, *WTF, Enjoy: Poems from Marc Maron's Newsletters*. He can often be found promoting philanthropy for non-profits in the Philadelphia area. His is on BlueSky social @poetphilly.bsky.social and X @PoetPhilly.

Made in the USA
Columbia, SC
07 January 2025

49799398R00048